The Special Needs Children

By: Sandra Gbotoe and Michelle S. Lazurek

This is a work of non-fiction. Names, characters, places, and incidents either are the product of the author's imagination or are used fictitiously. Any resemblance to actual persons, living or dead, events, or locales is entirely coincidental.

Book Design By Airris Books, Christine Racheal

ISBN 978-0-578-28371-5

Published by Sandra Gbotoe

www.sandragbotoe.com

Dedication

You were born to be a world changer!

Sandra Gbotoe

To special needs kids everywhere:

When you are weak, then you are strong.

Michelle S. Lazurek

Hi I'm Luna. I go to a special school because sometimes sounds and sights hurt my head. I wear my special pink glasses to help me see better.

My teacher helps me calm down
when loud sounds hurt my ears.

I hop off the school bus in the morning and run to my classroom. The first person I see is my friend, David. "Hi, David!" How are you?" "Hi Luna! I'm good," David swings his special chair - around to get a better look at me. "How are you?"

"Great! I had my favorite cereal this morning." Just then, the bell rang. Circle time! David and I made our way to sit down. David has to stay back from the circle because of his wheelchair.

We listened with our class as Mrs. Sullivan taught us math problems and then we made an art project using paper and glue.

Ick! The glue was sticky and got on my hands. I didn't get upset, though, I used a napkin to wipe it off.

Soon it was time for recess—my favorite part of the day! As we walked in a single file line out the door and onto the playground, Milo ran up to me.

"Hola, Luna! I like your glasses!"
"Hola! Thanks, I just got them."
"They look good. I had Mrs. Smith help me with my math again. I keep getting all the numbers mixed up in my head."
"That's OK. Mrs. Sullivan helps me calm down when I have to put my hands over my ears when it's too noisy. Hey, wanna see what Shannell is doing?"

Milo and I approached Shannell, who was in the corner of the playground, jumping up and down. She does that when she gets excited. She says it helps get all of her energy out.

"Hey, Shannell, how are you today?"

Shannell has a doll she holds onto to make her feel safe.

"Good, see the new outfit on my doll? I picked it out myself."

"It's pretty," I said, as I touched the hem of the white stitched dress Shannell's mom made by hand. It was soft when I touched it.

"Well, well, look at who we have here. It's the weird brigade." Maxine, one of the meanest kids in our school, started talking to us.

She ripped the doll out of Shannell's hands. "This is the ugliest dress I've ever seen!" Shannell started screaming and jumping up and down, hands flapping. "Give it back! Give it back!"

Maxine laughed. "You are so weird, Shannell. Why do you need this doll anyway? Aren't you, like, eight already? Dolls are for babies."

Shannell held out her hands grasping for the doll. One tear slipped down her cheek. She grabbed onto the doll's leg and ripped it from Maxine's hands, holding it close.

"Maxine, you are so mean! Leave her alone!" I shouted.

"OK, four eyes! Your glasses are so thick, it's any wonder you can even see me!" She turned and skipped off to play with her friends.

Just then, David noticed Maxine fall down as she was playing. His first thought was to let her lie on the ground. But then he thought it was better to be kind than to be mean. He went to help, but his chair only went as fast as he could push it. "Don't worry, David, I'll go!" I ran over to her.

"Here, Maxine, let me help." Maxine was stunned. She let me help her without saying a word. I was so glad David saw her fall. I was able to help when he couldn't.

Coming back inside from recess, someone had spilled water on the ground. "Watch out, Milo!" Shannell said to him.

He would have slipped if Shannell didn't warn him. Milo took Shannell's hands. That helped calm Shannell down.

"Want me to push your chair for you?" I offered David. The tight corners of the hallway make it hard for David to push his chair around. '

As everyone got back to their seats, they were talking too loudly, which hurt my ears. I put my hands over them to drown out the sound. "Quiet! SHHH!" David said aloud, placing his finger over his lips. He smiled at me from across the table. I looked to my right and noticed Shannell helping Milo with his math again.

Just then, I thought how lucky I am to have such good friends. I can run for David when he gets tired from pushing his chair. David helped my ears not to hurt when he quieted everyone down. Shannell helped Milo with his math, and Milo helped calm Shannell down coming in from recess.

' Sure, we may go to a special school, but that's OK! When we use our weaknesses to help each other, we spread kindness and love to the world, showing everyone being different is pretty special after all.

SCHOOl

Made in the USA
Columbia, SC
26 June 2025

59929465R00018